THE DEPARTMENT OF ENERGY

A LOOK BEHIND THE SCENES

By Michael Burgan

Content Consultant:
Sanya Carley, PhD
Associate Professor
School of Public and Environmental Affairs
Indiana University
Bloomington, Indiana

COMPASS POINT BOOKS
a capstone imprint

Compass Point Books are published by Capstone
1710 Roe Crest Drive, North Mankato, Minnesota 56003
www.mycapstone.com

Library of Congress Cataloging-in-Publication Data
Names: Burgan, Michael, author.
Title: The Department of Energy : a look behind the scenes / by Michael Burgan.
Description: North Mankato, MN : Compass Point Books, [2019] | Series: U.S. government behind the scenes | Includes bibliographical references and index. | Audience: Ages 12-17.
Identifiers: LCCN 2018042026 (print) | LCCN 2018048947 (ebook) | ISBN 9780756559137 (ebook PDF) | ISBN 9780756559007 (hardcover) | ISBN 9780756559090 (pbk.)
Subjects: LCSH: United States. Department of Energy—Juvenile literature. | Energy policy—United States—Juvenile literature.
Classification: LCC HD9502.U52 (ebook) | LCC HD9502.U52 B865 2019 (print) | DDC 333.790973—dc23
LC record available at https://lccn.loc.gov/2018042026

Summary: It takes a lot of power to run a country. Whether it's fossil fuels, nuclear energy, or renewable energy sources, the Department of Energy oversees them all. One of 15 departments within the executive branch, the Department of Energy relies on scientists and experts in many fields to manage the energy needs of the United States. Should we use nuclear or renewable energy? Should we restrict the places where we drill for oil? The department investigates these questions and more. From its early days as a department designed to secure our fuel needs, its responsibilities have grown to include ensuring the nation's security and prosperity through the power of energy.

Editorial Credits:
Amy Kortuem, editor; Terri Poburka, designer; Jo Miller, media researcher Tori Abraham, production specialist

Image Credits:
Alamy: Dino Fracchia, 42, National Geographic Creative, 15, Science History Images, 23; AP Images: John Duricka, 33; Getty Images: Bettmann/Contributor, 28, J.R. Eyerman/Contributor, 19, Jeff T. Green/Stringer, 44, Popperfoto/Contributor, 25, Time Life Pictures/ Contributor, 39, Wally McNamee/Contributor, 51; Glow Images: Deposit Photos, 21; Newscom: Blend Images/Hill Street Studios, 57, Cover Images/Dept. of Energy's Oak Ridge National Laboratory/Carlos Jones, 6, Everett Collection, 26, Minden Pictures/ Michio Hoshino, 52, ZUMA Press/Los Alamos National Laboratory, 12, ZUMA Press/Simon Edelman, 4, ZUMA Press/SSGT Alan R. Wycheck, 35; Oak Ridge National Laboratory, 7; Science Source: Argonne National Laboratory, 9, DOE/NNSA, 37; Shutterstock: iofoto, 55, Jose L Vilchez, Cover, Kyle T Perry, 53, LagunaticPhoto, 45, petch one, 16-17, Serhii Bobyk, 5; Wikimedia: US Department of Energy, 47

Design Elements:
Shutterstock: anndypit, ben Bryant, RetroClipArt, Tobias Steinert

Printed and bound in the USA.
PA49

TABLE OF CONTENTS

CHAPTER ONE

Energy in Many Forms

Watching an animated movie, the audience might not realize the immense computing power that was needed to make it. That power makes details such as strands of hair look lifelike. Movie companies such as Pixar and DreamWorks are eagerly watching the development of a new generation of supercomputers. The computers will let their artists create even richer detail in their work. The money funding the development of these "exascale" computers comes in part from the U.S. Department of Energy (DOE).

But making great movies is not why the DOE is funding these computers. With its Exascale Computing Project (ECP), the DOE hopes to use the new super-fast computers to help government experts do their jobs better. The new computers, for example, could help DOE scientists find ways to increase the power generated by wind turbines. Branches of the government that fight terrorism could also use the new computers to more quickly analyze the information gathered on possible terrorists. An exacomputer could also help predict the effects of climate changes on crops and help develop treatments for some cancers.

Businesses will also benefit from the vastly increased computing speed. For example, the exacomputers will help auto companies design lighter cars that use less fuel, while remaining strong enough to protect passengers during a crash. Many aspects of science and technology require fast computer calculations, and the new supercomputers will speed up the process.

In 2017 the DOE gave six U.S. companies more than $258 million to carry out research on the ECP. The companies also pledged money to the project and will work with scientists at six national laboratories. The labs are part of a group of 17 run by the Department of Energy.

Movie companies will use exacomputers in the future to make animations and special effects look even more realistic.

In June 2018 the Department of Energy's Oak Ridge National Laboratory introduced Summit, the world's fastest supercomputer.

The scientists involved in the project have several challenges as they work to build an exascale computer. Extremely fast computers require large amounts of electricity to run. They must also be cooled so they don't break down. Exacomputers will need more power and cooling than any other computers ever made. The new computers will also require new software. Finally, the U.S. scientists are trying to catch up with computer experts in China. That country has some of the world's fastest supercomputers. In 2017 it announced that its first exascale computer would be operating in 2020. China and the United States often compete around the world for influence in business and military affairs. The country with the fastest computers can have an advantage in processing information it needs to pursue its interests. Some U.S. lawmakers want to see the United States regain the lead it once had in consistently producing the world's fastest computers.

Measuring Computing Power

The name exascale refers to the number of calculations per second the new supercomputers will perform. The first computer was introduced in 1946 and could add 5,000 numbers per second. Today, the fastest U.S. supercomputer can do quadrillions of calculations per second. Written as a number, one quadrillion looks like this: 1,000,000,000,000,000. One quadrillion calculations per second is known as a petaflop. *Peta* comes from a Greek word meaning "five" and refers to the fact that one quadrillion is the same as 1,000 multiplied by itself five times. In 2017, the world's fastest computer, in China, could do 93 petaflops. In 2018, the DOE began operating a computer at the Oak Ridge National Lab with a speed of 200 petaflops. Exascale computers will reach speeds of 1,000 petaflops. That's one trillion times faster than today's laptops. *Exa* comes from a Greek word meaning "six" and refers to the fact that one quintillion, the next large number measurement after a quadrillion, is the same as 1,000 multiplied by itself six times.

Oak Ridge National Laboratory in Tennessee

For the DOE in particular, increased computing power will have many benefits. The department already controls the fastest supercomputers in the United States, which are kept at some of the national labs. Current supercomputers are used to help DOE and other government scientists carry out experiments, called simulations. The simulations show what could happen in different situations. For example, a supercomputer can help study what materials might be best for a certain energy project. The simulation provides useful information without the cost of actually buying the materials and carrying out a physical experiment. One DOE supercomputer was used in 2018 to carry out simulations about earthquakes. From the simulation, scientists learned how an earthquake in a specific part of San Francisco would affect nearby buildings.

A Department's Mission

The work that the DOE does relies heavily on scientists who are experts in such fields as physics, biology, and chemistry. Some of their work is concerned with making sure the United States has enough energy to meet its needs. At the same time, scientists work to reduce any possible negative impacts the production of energy has on people and the environment. The department is also in charge of building and maintaining the nation's nuclear weapons. These weapons are the most destructive in the world. They have only been used twice in history, both times in 1945 at the end of World War II. Most people hope they are never used again. But the DOE makes sure the U.S. military will have nuclear weapons that work properly if they are ever needed.

The Department of Energy is one of 15 executive departments in the U.S. government. The mission of the DOE is to "to ensure America's security and prosperity by addressing its energy, environmental and nuclear challenges through transformative science and technology solutions."

To carry out its mission the department's different offices focus on several basic areas related to energy. Along with building nuclear weapons, some parts of the DOE work to make sure those weapons don't end up in the hands of groups that might want to harm the United States. Nuclear energy is also used to power some plants that generate electricity. The department has a role in promoting the safe use of that power. The DOE also makes sure the United States has the energy it needs for generating electricity and transporting goods and people. Part of that effort means trying to expand the production of fossil fuels—oil, coal, and natural gas. DOE scientists also work to develop alternatives to fossil fuels, such as biofuels from organic materials, or electric or fuel cell vehicles. The department also promotes the development of renewable energy, such as water, solar, and wind energy. Using these sources of energy reduces the production of so-called greenhouse gases, which are linked to the global warming of Earth. This warming is also called climate change, and scientists predict it may lead to coastal flooding, among other environmental problems.

A technician at DOE's Argonne National Laboratory tested the all-electric Tesla Roadster to gather data on electric cars.

Given its important role in funding and carrying out scientific research in many fields, the DOE often works with other executive departments. Because of its work on nuclear weapons, the department has close ties to the Department of Defense on some projects. The DOE also works with executive agencies, such as the Environmental Protection Agency (EPA). Together, the DOE and the EPA put in place standards for the U.S. fuel economy and greenhouse gas emissions. They provide information on which cars get the best gas mileage and on cars that use batteries for some or all of their power. The DOE is also an important source of money and information for the states. Among other projects, the DOE helps the states reduce their use of fossil fuels and rely more on renewable energy sources. The department's Office of Science also gives public and private colleges money to conduct research. Much of the research funded by the DOE goes on at the 17 national laboratories it runs.

Where the Energy Comes From

Here are the major sources of the nation's energy, as of 2016:

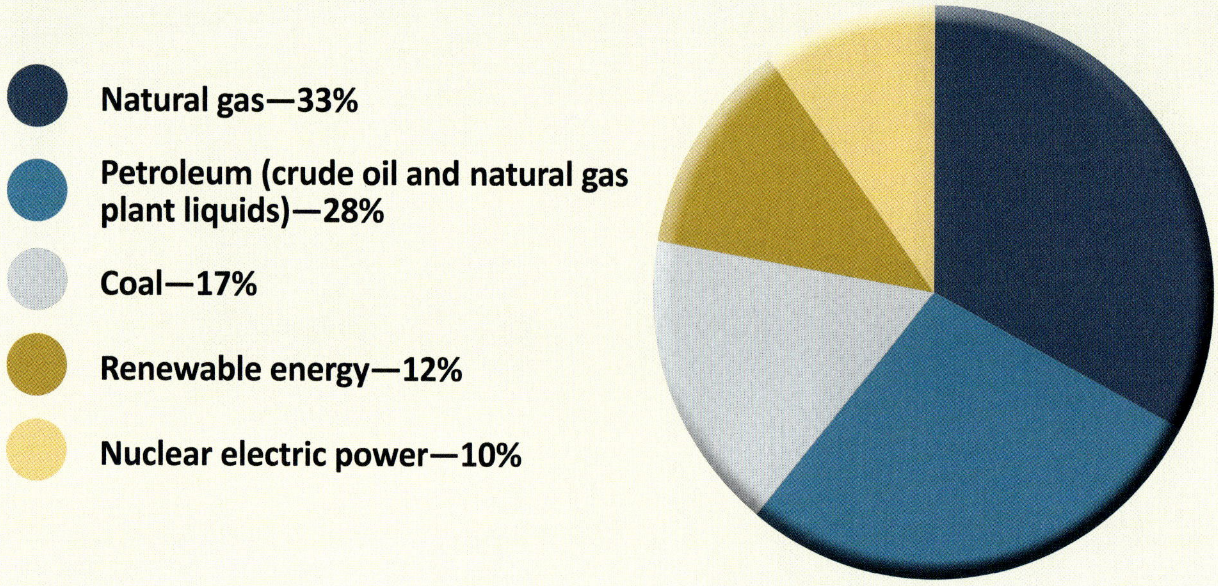

Where the Money Goes

These DOE programs received the most money in the 2018 budget:

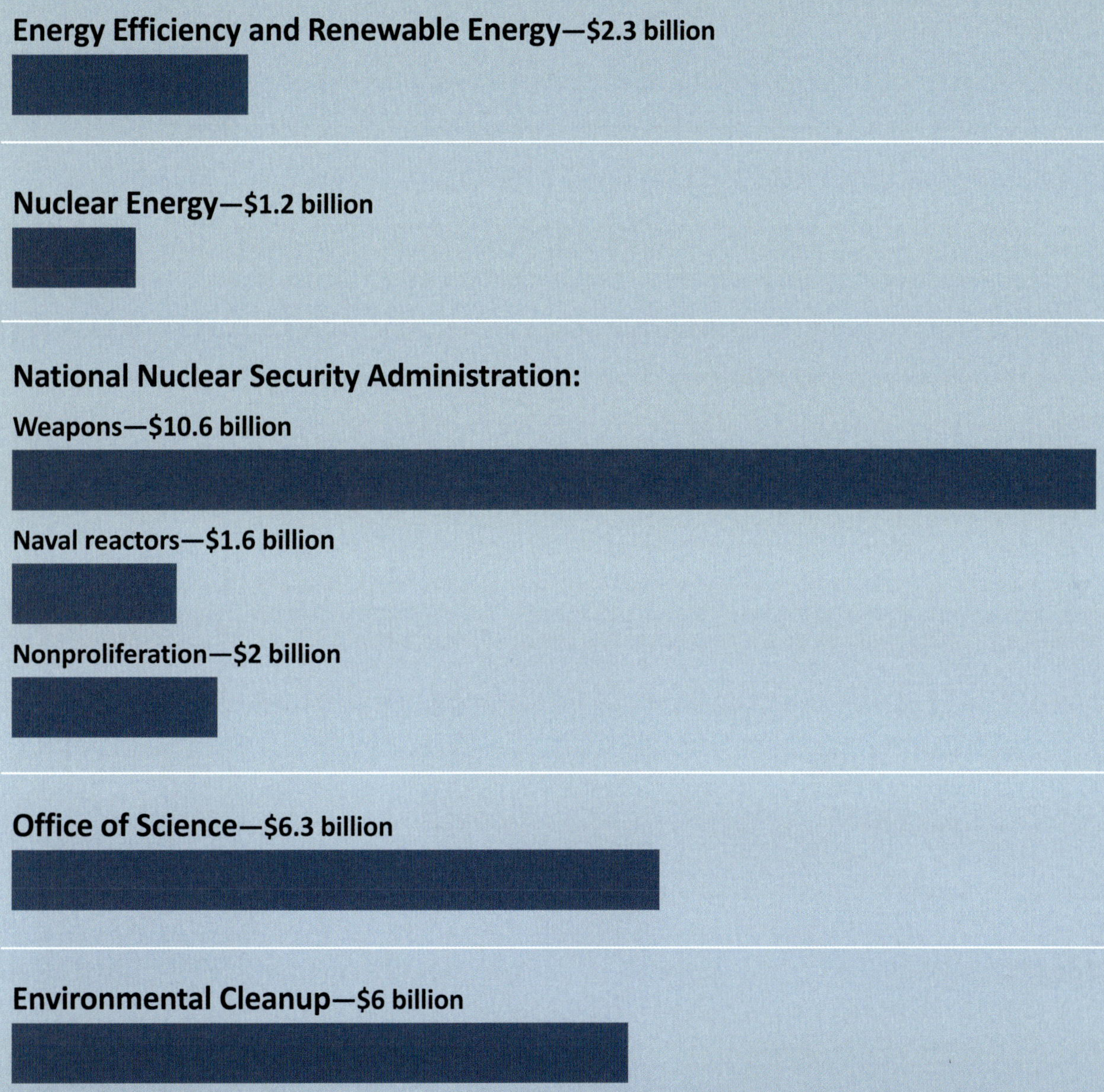

Training Young Scientists

Along with carrying out research, the national labs encourage college students to learn more about science and technology. At Los Alamos National Laboratory in New Mexico, students can take part in a variety of summer programs. One is designed to help young women become engineers. Others focus on computers or space science. At Argonne National Laboratory in Illinois, students can study cybersecurity. These are efforts to keep computer networks free from outside attacks that can steal data or shut down the system. The educational programs at Brookhaven National Laboratory in New York also include some high school students. Recent projects there ranged from a study of bumblebees to the use of nanomaterials. These are materials thousands of times smaller than the width of a single strand of human hair. Another project at Brookhaven was focused on bringing more African Americans and other minorities into science. Quentarius Moore of Mississippi had never heard of Brookhaven before taking part in the project. After, he said, "Now I hope to help minority students seek similar learning experiences."

Los Alamos National Laboratory in New Mexico

The Duties of the Department

The head of the Department of Energy is the secretary of Energy. The secretary is one member of the president's cabinet—the top advisors he or she turns to when deciding what policies to pursue. The president may also choose to have the secretary of Energy be a member of the National Security Council. The council advises the president on all issues relating to the nation's security and foreign affairs. After a president chooses a secretary, the Senate must approve the choice, as it does with other executive department leaders.

The secretary of Energy directs the department's general operations. The deputy secretary helps run the department, which has about 106,000 employees and contractors. One of the deputy's major duties is supervising the work of the many contractors the DOE hires to help carry out its work. The contractors include universities and private companies. A large percentage of the money the department receives each year goes to pay contractors. They run most of the national labs for the DOE. The labs perform a wide range of duties. Along with running the supercomputers used for research, various labs work on developing new nuclear weapons, studying the climate, and developing new sources of energy, such as more powerful batteries.

The main duties of the DOE are carried out by three major divisions, called offices. Each office is led by an undersecretary. The Office of Nuclear Security and National Nuclear Security Administration handles all of the DOE's responsibilities regarding nuclear weapons. It also oversees the program that provides nuclear power for some U.S. naval ships and submarines. The Office of Science is in charge of the different research the department sponsors. It spends more money on basic research in physical sciences than any other U.S. agency. Physical science pertains to the nature of matter and energy. The office has several smaller offices within it, including one that handles the cleanup of sites related to past nuclear weapons programs. The third DOE office is the Office of Energy. Its different divisions address such topics as conserving energy, developing renewable energy and fossil fuels, and ensuring energy supplies for the nation's American Indian tribes.

Fifteen smaller offices and agencies within the DOE are separate from these three main offices. They oversee such programs as the production of electricity through a large network of dams and the general operation of the DOE as a whole. Together, the different agencies within the DOE have a broad responsibility to carry out cutting-edge scientific research and make sure the United States always has the energy it needs.

A physicist conducted research at Argonne National Laboratory, which is funded by the DOE.

Map of Department of Energy Laboratories

Office of Science Laboratories

1. Ames Laboratory
   Ames, Iowa
2. Argonne National Laboratory
   Argonne, Illinois
3. Brookhaven National Laboratory
   Upton, New York
4. Fermi National Accelerator Laboratory
   Batavia, Illinois
5. Lawrence Berkeley National Laboratory
   Berkeley, California
6. Oak Ridge National Laboratory
   Oak Ridge, Tennessee
7. Pacific Northwest National Laboratory
   Richland, Washington
8. Princeton Plasma Physics Laboratory
   Princeton, New Jersey
9. SLAC National Accelerator Laboratory
   Menlo Park, California
10. Thomas Jefferson National Accelerator Facility
    Newport News, Virginia

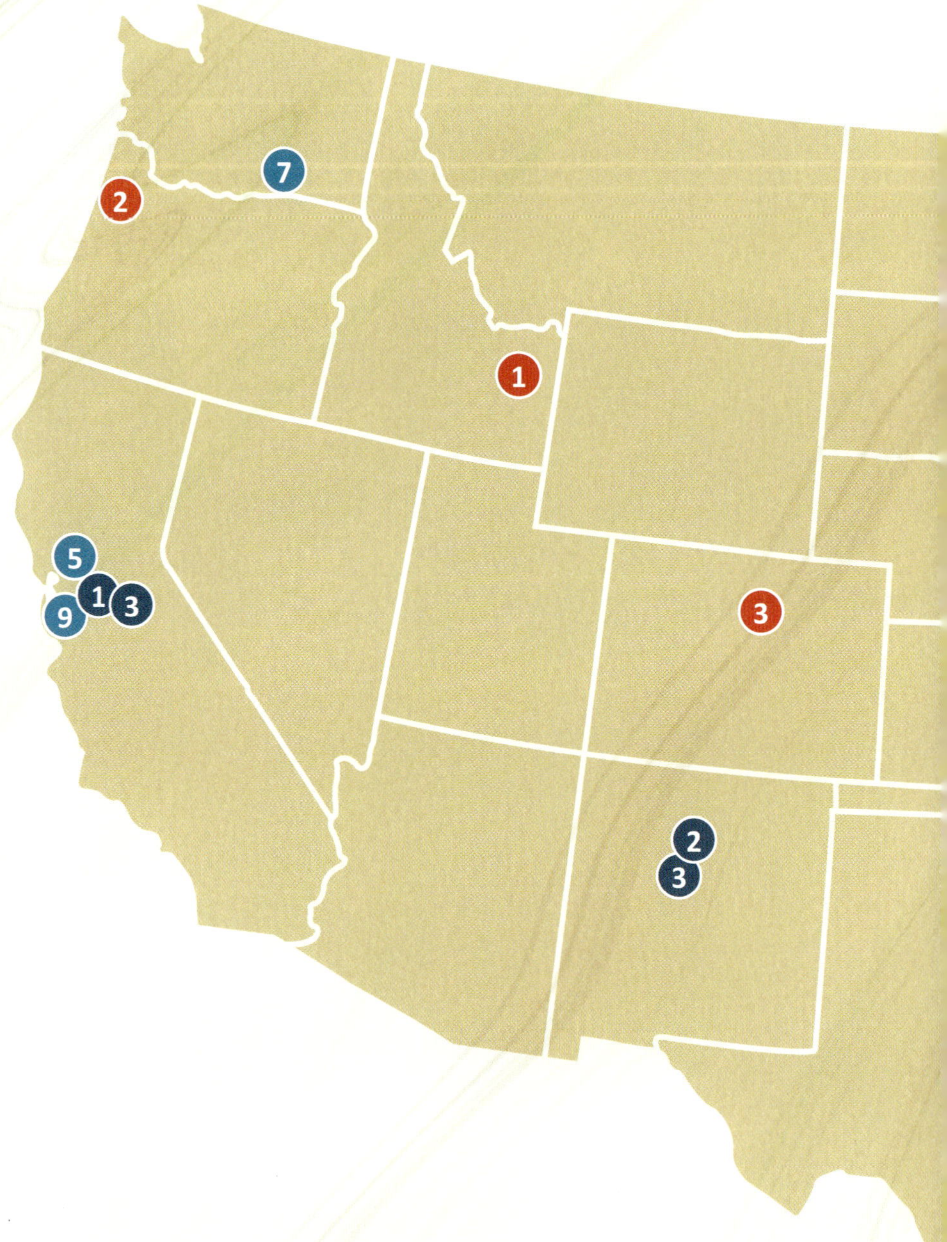

Other DOE Laboratories

1. Idaho National Laboratory
   Idaho Falls, Idaho
2. National Energy Technology Laboratory
   Morgantown, West Virginia; Pittsburgh, Pennsylvania; Albany, Oregon
3. National Renewable Energy Laboratory
   Golden, Colorado
4. Savannah River National Laboratory
   Aiken, South Carolina

National Nuclear Security Administration (NNSA) Laboratories

1. Lawrence Livermore National Laboratory
   Livermore, California
2. Los Alamos National Laboratory
   Los Alamos, New Mexico
3. Sandia National Laboratory
   Albuquerque, New Mexico; Livermore, California

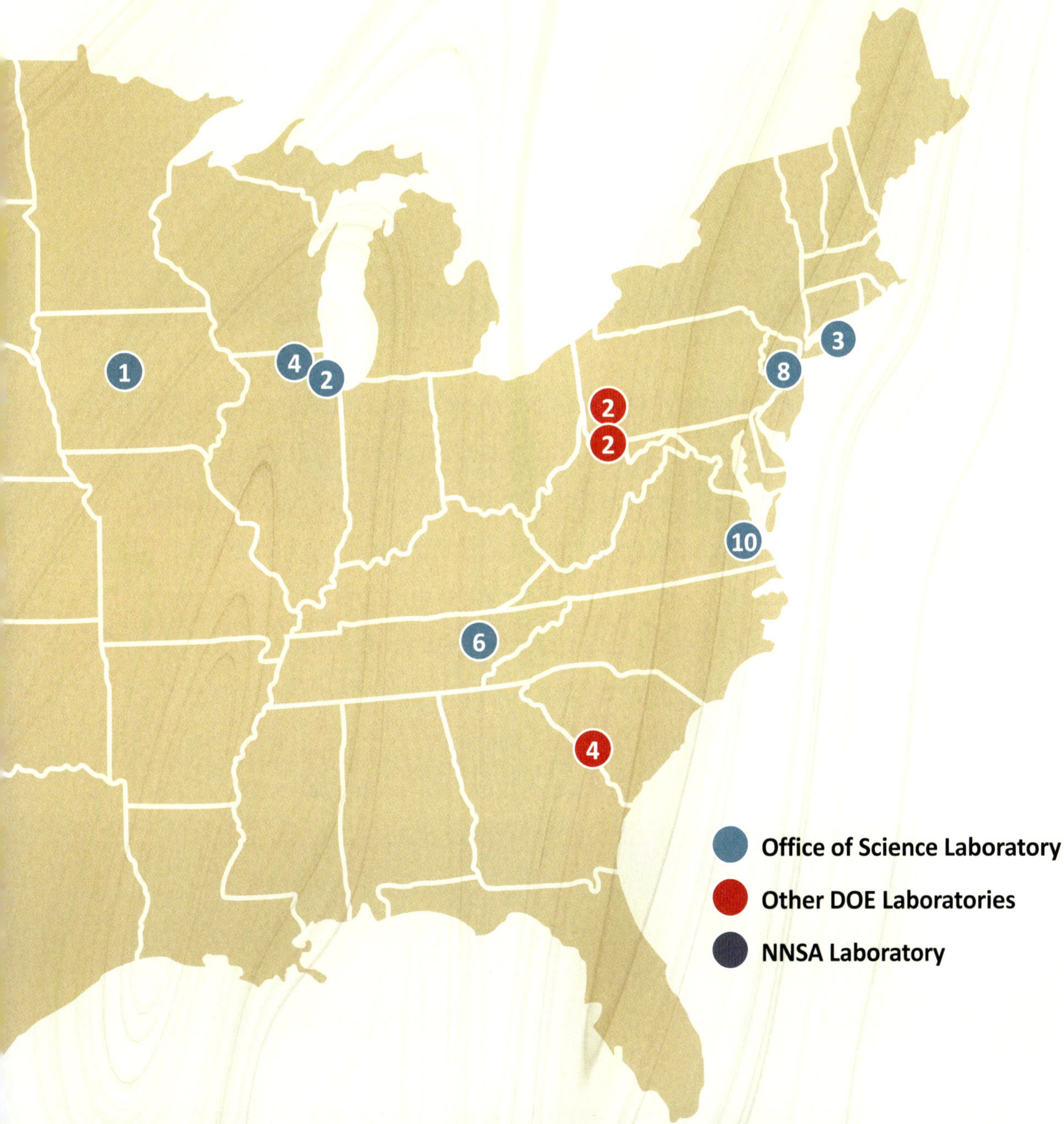

CHAPTER TWO

The Road to Creating the Department of Energy

When European settlers came to America, they relied on wood to fuel fires for cooking and heat. At early mills and factories, the energy created by rushing rivers provided the power to run basic machinery. Even before the settlers came, American Indians across North America had found other natural resources that could be used for fuel. The Hopi Indians used coal for fires to make pottery. Other tribes across the continent found spots where oil and natural gas came out of the ground and reached the surface. The Hopi used the oil for medicine and to waterproof canoes, among other uses.

During the 19th century, coal became the main source of energy for the United States. Starting in the 20th century, the use of natural gas and oil—also called petroleum—began to rise. U.S. coal mines and oil wells helped fuel the nation's growth as a major industrial nation. Private companies did most of the work to locate and produce the fuels that powered machinery, railroads, cars, and the plants that generated electricity.

Shale oil miners used machines to probe into the rock walls to retrieve petroleum.

The U.S. government began to take a more active role in energy issues at the beginning of the 20th century. In 1910 it created the Bureau of Mines as part of the Department of the Interior. The bureau's mission was to try to improve safety conditions for coal miners. The government also wanted to ensure it had enough petroleum to power naval ships. Starting in 1909, the government set aside public lands where it could drill for oil for the navy. Today's Office of Fossil Energy in the DOE traces its roots to those efforts.

The Bureau of Mines was also interested in oil production. In 1918 it opened what was called an experimental station in Bartlesville, Oklahoma. The bureau's goal was to find better ways to extract and process petroleum into fuel and other products. This station and two other experimental stations that focused on coal research eventually became the National Energy Technology Laboratory. It is one of the Department of Energy's national labs.

In 1920 the U.S. government turned its attention to a renewable energy source: water. It created the Federal Power Commission (FPC) to supervise the construction of hydroelectric projects. The commission was run by three executive departments: Agriculture, Interior, and War (now called the Defense Department). During the 1930s, the FPC became an independent federal agency and its role increased, as it also regulated the sale of natural gas and electricity.

Also during the 1930s, scientists in various countries realized that the world could soon have a new source of energy. They knew that the atoms of certain materials contained great amounts of energy. Splitting those atoms would release that energy. In 1938 two German scientists discovered a process called nuclear fission. They bombarded the nucleus, or core, of uranium atoms with tiny particles called neutrons. This process split the atoms, releasing more neutrons and energy.

Other scientists quickly realized that the energy released from nuclear fission could be used in two important ways. It could be used to boil water to create steam that could then power ships or plants that generate electricity. Nuclear power could also be used to create weapons with tremendous destructive power. One scientific study in 1941 suggested that just 25 pounds (11.3 kg) of uranium could create the same explosive force as 1,800 tons (1,633 tonnes) of dynamite. Nuclear weapons would also release radiation, a form of energy that can kill people in large doses.

The Good and Bad of Radiation

Earth and everything on it is surrounded by various forms of energy. Light and radio waves are some examples of this energy. So is radiation. Many common items such as rocks and plants emit small amounts of radiation. The human body does too. In low doses, radiation is not harmful. It has positive uses. X-rays and some treatments for cancer rely on radiation. Radioactive materials can also be used to determine the age of ancient objects. In large doses, however, radiation can cause sickness or death. Scientists have worked out formulas that outline how much radiation people can be exposed to over a certain length of time before they increase their risk of health problems. Protective gear, such as gas masks and special clothing, can also reduce the exposure to radiation. The Department of Energy works to make sure that radioactive materials used at the national labs do not release large amounts of radiation that could harm workers or people who live near the labs.

The Nuclear Energy Race

In September 1939 Germany began World War II by invading Poland. The United States did not enter the war until December 1941. Japan attacked the United States in December 1941 at Pearl Harbor, Hawaii. Japan sided with Germany in the war. The Pearl Harbor attack brought the United States into the war against both of those countries. Since the start of the war, even before the attack in Hawaii, President Franklin Roosevelt knew that the United States would probably have to battle the Germans. He did not want Germany to build a nuclear weapon bomb before the United States did. Just a single nuclear bomb could wipe out an entire U.S. city. In October 1939 Roosevelt set up a committee to study the possibility of developing what would be called the atomic bomb. That effort was later called the Manhattan Project. Research and bomb development took place at various sites across the United States.

The U.S. military was in charge of the Manhattan Project. It successfully tested the world's first atomic bomb in a New Mexico desert in July 1945. Several weeks later the United States dropped two of the bombs on Japan. The two atomic devices dropped on Japan killed more than 100,000 people instantly. Tens of thousands more died from radiation. On August 14, after the second bombing, Japan announced it was ready to surrender.

After the war, Congress realized that nuclear energy had both peaceful and military uses. President Harry Truman signed the Atomic Energy Act of 1946. That year Congress created the Atomic Energy Commission (AEC), which put the research of nuclear energy under civilian control rather than military. The commission oversaw the development of nuclear weapons and stressed security

The Shippingport Atomic Power Station in Pennsylvania was the world's first atomic power plant dedicated to peacetime nuclear energy needs.

measures to prevent the Soviet Union from learning about U.S. weapons. The Americans and Soviets had fought together against the Germans, but tensions were rising. The two countries were now struggling for supremacy as they tried to spread their military and political influence around the world. This struggle to win influence came to be called the Cold War. The AEC and U.S. leaders did not realize in 1946 the amount of information the Soviet Union had collected about nuclear weapons from spies working on the Manhattan Project. The Soviets were already on their way to building their own atomic bomb. Each country would then compete to build more nuclear weapons than the other. By the 1950s the two countries had developed even more destructive nuclear weapons. The weapons' deadly force came from joining together, or fusing, hydrogen atoms, using radiation released from splitting uranium atoms.

Nuclear power also became important for the navies of both nations. The United States launched the world's first nuclear submarine, the *Nautilus*, in 1954. The sub could stay underwater for weeks without having to refuel because of its nuclear-powered engine. A branch of the AEC built the nuclear power system for the *Nautilus*.

The AEC also explored using nuclear power to generate electricity. President Dwight D. Eisenhower promoted this "Atoms for Peace" program, in part to compete with the Soviet Union and other nations in the push to build commercial nuclear reactors. That effort received a boost when Congress passed the Atomic Energy Act of 1954. The law gave private companies the right to research peaceful uses of nuclear power. The AEC would enforce safety regulations to prevent accidents that could cause explosions and release radiation.

Using a reactor similar to the one that powered the *Nautilus*, in 1957 the AEC opened a commercial nuclear power plant outside Pittsburgh, Pennsylvania, to generate electricity. By the early 1960s two U.S. companies were designing and building reactors for commercial use. Companies were building generating plants without any government funding. The AEC, however, remained in charge of guaranteeing that they ran safely. The commission was also still involved with the building and testing of nuclear weapons. They worked with the Department of Defense and private contractors.

The Nautilus, *the world's first nuclear-powered submarine, was used by the US Navy until 1980.*

Since the Manhattan Project, the United States had tested its nuclear weapons by exploding them at remote sites. The tests, though, released vast amounts of radiation into the air that drifted all over Earth. The radiation posed a risk to humans, especially babies, if they drank milk that came from cows exposed to a particularly deadly form of the radiation. Some adults developed cancers related to exposure to the radiation. Radioactive materials also entered the oceans and harmed some sea creatures. In 1963 the Unites States, the Soviet Union, and Great Britain signed a treaty that outlawed nuclear tests above ground, in the water, or in outer space. The countries would test their weapons only underground. The AEC had already been carrying out underground testing in Nevada. It continued to do so. Even with the underground tests, some radiation escaped into the atmosphere or underground sources of water, meaning they could pose a threat to human health.

President Kennedy signed the Nuclear Test Ban Treaty in 1963.

Powering a Nation

While the AEC was focused on nuclear energy in different forms, the U.S. government still lacked one cabinet-level department that oversaw all the nation's energy concerns. President Richard Nixon tried to change that. In 1971 he called for the creation of a Department of Natural Resources. It would take on the duties of some existing departments and agencies, such as the AEC. One of the new department's goals would be to ensure a supply of fuels to meet the nation's energy needs. Nixon outlined his concern about energy resources later that year. For the first time, a president sent a message to Congress addressing energy concerns. Nixon noted that some parts of the nation had experienced shortages of electricity. Prices for oil, coal, and natural had increased. Nixon said, "We cannot take our energy supply for granted any longer. A sufficient supply of clean energy is essential if we are to sustain healthy economic growth and improve the quality of our national life."

His proposals included allowing more extraction of energy resources on federal lands, research into new forms of energy production, and having his planned Department of Natural Resources oversee all the different programs related to energy resource development.

Although Congress did not create the new department that Nixon wanted, the nation soon saw energy issues become a major concern. The United States increasingly relied on oil produced in the Middle East for gasoline for cars, boats, planes and other moving vehicles. Most of the leaders of the Middle Eastern nations were Arabs. They opposed American military support for Israel. The Arabs of the region and the Israelis had battled each other several times since the nation of Israel was created in 1948. In October 1973, several Arab nations attacked Israel. President Nixon promised the Israelis more military aid. In response, the Arab oil-producing states stopped selling oil to the United States and other countries friendly with Israel. This embargo led gas prices to shoot up quickly. Drivers sometimes had to wait in line for hours to fill up their gas tanks.

People lined up for gas in California on the first day of gas rationing, 1979.

In November 1973 Nixon spoke to the nation about the gas crisis and the nation's future energy needs. Nixon said Americans had to find ways to use less energy. They had to reduce their reliance on fuel that came from foreign nations. The next month the president created the Federal Energy Office (FEO) to deal with the oil embargo. This was soon followed by the Federal Energy Administration (FEA). It took on the duties of the FEO as well as some activities related to energy sources that had previously been done by the Department of the Interior.

More changes were underway in how the federal government addressed energy issues. In 1974 Congress ended the AEC and split its duties between two new agencies. The Nuclear Regulatory Commission (NRC) ensured the safe operation of nuclear power plants and other uses of radioactive material. The Energy Research and Development Administration (ERDA) focused on nuclear weapons and research on new sources of energy. It took over the national labs that had performed research for the AEC.

Petroleum by the Barrel

U.S. petroleum consumption in millions of barrels per day, 1950 to 1980

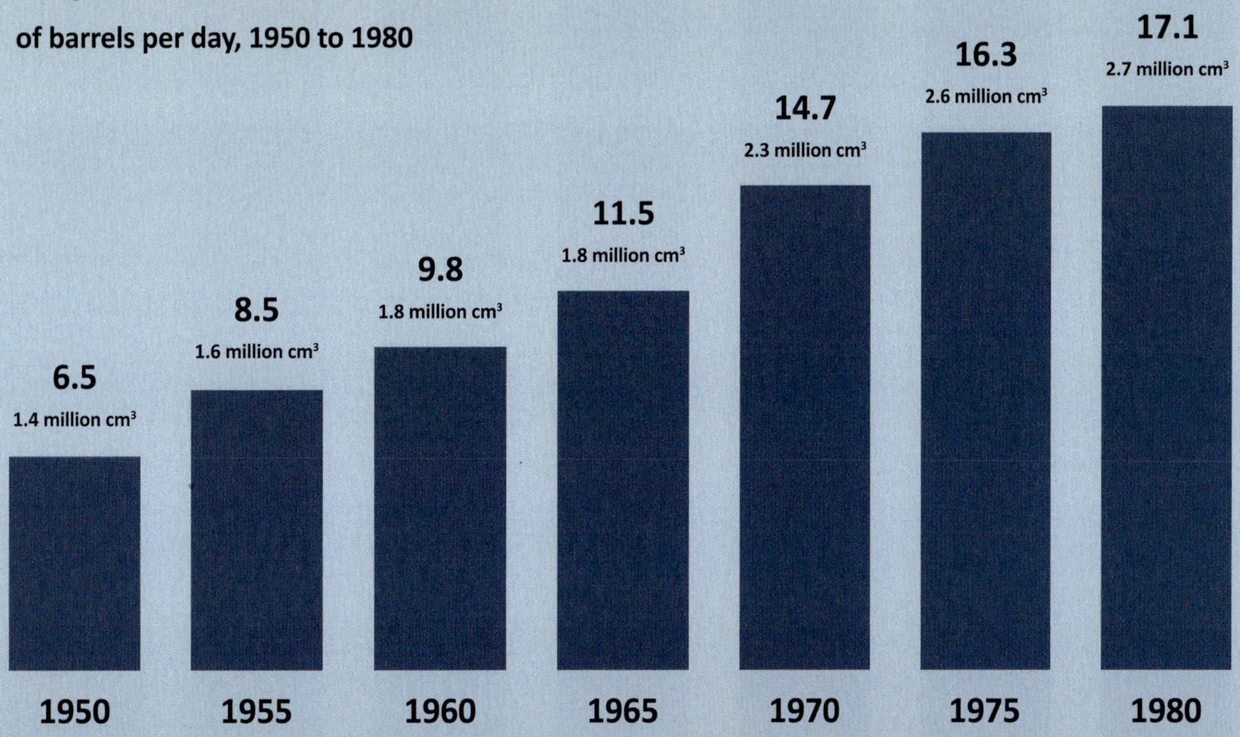

The increased focus on energy production and use finally led to the creation of the Department of Energy in 1977. Before he left office, President Gerald Ford called for creating that cabinet-level department. Incoming president Jimmy Carter supported its creation as well. Carter took office with the nation facing a shortage of natural gas, which was used to heat many homes and businesses. In March he sent Congress his plan for creating a Department of Energy. Carter saw, like Nixon before him, that the nation was relying more and more on foreign sources of energy. That meant other nations could influence how much fuel Americans got and how much they paid for it. Carter wanted to reduce energy use while turning to coal, nuclear power, and renewable sources for more of the nation's needs.

Congress quickly agreed to Carter's request for a new department. The Department of Energy (DOE) began operating in October 1977. It took over the functions of the FEA, the ERDA, the Federal Power Commission, and energy-related responsibilities from other executive departments. The Federal Energy Regulatory Commission was set up as an independent agency within the DOE. It took over many of the duties of the old Federal Power Commission. Some duties were overseeing and regulating interstate electricity, natural gas, oil trades, and hydroelectric projects.

At its creation the DOE had about 20,000 employees and a budget of about $10.5 billion. One department goal was to research new fuel sources and find practical uses for them. Given the fuel shortages and price hikes of the 1970s, President Carter said the department would also "make sure that consumers of our nation are treated fairly, that prices are adequate and not excessive."

Big Energy Worries

Soon after the creation of the DOE, officials wrestled with several energy-related problems. Another gasoline shortage hit the United States in 1979. Carter called for Americans to use less energy. He also promoted the increased use of solar power.

Also in 1979 an accident at the Three Mile Island nuclear power plant in Pennsylvania damaged one of the two reactors there. This led to the release of some radiation. For a time government officials worried about even more radiation escaping the plant. The Nuclear Regulatory Commission was in charge of overseeing nuclear power plants. The DOE also played a role in handling the crisis. Employees from Brookhaven National Laboratory's Radiological Assistance Program (RAP) Team were among the first U.S. government experts on the scene. The DOE also sent helicopters to the area to measure levels of radiation in the air. The accident raised fears among some Americans about the safety of using nuclear power to generate electricity. But DOE secretary James Schlesinger said the nation needed nuclear power to make sure it had enough energy. After the accident, nuclear waste from the damaged plant was stored at the DOE's National Engineering Laboratory in Idaho.

During its first few years the DOE was often criticized. Some Americans believed that the department's rules made it hard for private energy companies to make money and find new sources of fuel. One of the critics was Ronald Reagan. He defeated Carter in the 1980 presidential election. President Reagan and some of his supporters called for getting rid of the DOE. In the end, Reagan decided to keep the department. But he did not have it play a large role in trying to control energy costs, as it had under Carter. The DOE would still carry out important scientific research related to energy. It would try to increase production of fossil fuels on federal lands.

The First Secretary

When he signed the law that created the Department of Energy, President Jimmy Carter picked James Schlesinger to be its first secretary. Schlesinger had been advising Carter on energy issues since Carter took office in January 1977. Schlesinger had trained as an economist and came to Washington in 1969 to help address how the federal government took in and spent money. President Richard Nixon later named him secretary of the Defense Department, and Schlesinger held that job for a little more than two years. He also served for a time as head of the Atomic Energy Commission and the Central Intelligence Agency. On energy issues, Schlesinger believed the United States had to prepare for the day when supplies of fossil fuel began to run out. That led him to call for using more nuclear energy. But he also wanted the United States to get more of its power from coal so it would not have to rely on oil from foreign countries. During the oil shortage of 1979, Carter and Schlesinger received some of the blame for the problems. As Carter lost popularity, he decided to change some of the members of his cabinet. Schlesinger left the DOE in July 1979.

President Jimmy Carter (right) appointed his energy adviser, James Schlesinger, to lead the newly formed DOE.

CHAPTER THREE

The Department at Work

In the African nation of Ghana in 2017, Chinese scientists carefully lowered a new source of fuel into a nuclear reactor. The Ghanaians use the reactor to conduct experiments. The type of fuel Ghana used before 2017 contained high levels of uranium that could be used to make nuclear weapons. The fuel worried nuclear experts in the United States and around the world. If terrorists had ever gotten any of the highly enriched uranium in the fuel, they could have used it to make small nuclear weapons. The new fuel uses low-enriched uranium, which can't be used to make weapons.

Reducing the amount of highly enriched uranium used at research reactors is one goal of the National Nuclear Security Administration (NNSA). Created in 2000, the NNSA is an independent agency within the Department of Energy. Its budget in 2017 was almost $13 billion. This is more than one-third of the department's total budget. Trying to keep nuclear materials out of the hands of terrorists is just one of the NNSA's important jobs.

The NNSA has worked with China and international organizations to get rid of highly enriched uranium. In Ghana NNSA scientists first made sure the reactor there could run on the less-dangerous form of uranium. Then they worked with the Chinese to make the fuel switch. In recent years the NNSA has helped remove all the potentially dangerous uranium from more than 30 countries. They removed a total of almost 7 tons (6.4 tonnes) of the radioactive material. While China and the United States are often political rivals, their scientists have worked together over the past decade to stop the illegal spread of nuclear fuel. A lab in China got some of its high-tech equipment from the NNSA. The lab is devoted to finding nuclear fuel before it can be smuggled.

The Minuteman III *is the only land-based intercontinental ballistic missile still in service in the United States.*

Dealing with nuclear weapons and the materials used to make them forms a large part of the NNSA's mission. During the height of the Cold War in the 1960s the United States had more than 30,000 nuclear warheads, which are the explosive end of a weapon. Some of the warheads were on missiles that could be launched from submarines or larger rockets stored in the ground. Others were bombs, while smaller warheads could be fired by weapons on a battlefield. During the 1970s and 1980s, the United States and the Soviet Union made several agreements to greatly reduce the number of nuclear weapons they deployed, or had ready for immediate use. They also reduced the number of warheads they stockpiled, or kept ready for use. After the Soviet Union split apart, Russia, which had ruled Soviet nations, continued to honor those agreements.

U.S. Nuclear Warheads, 2017

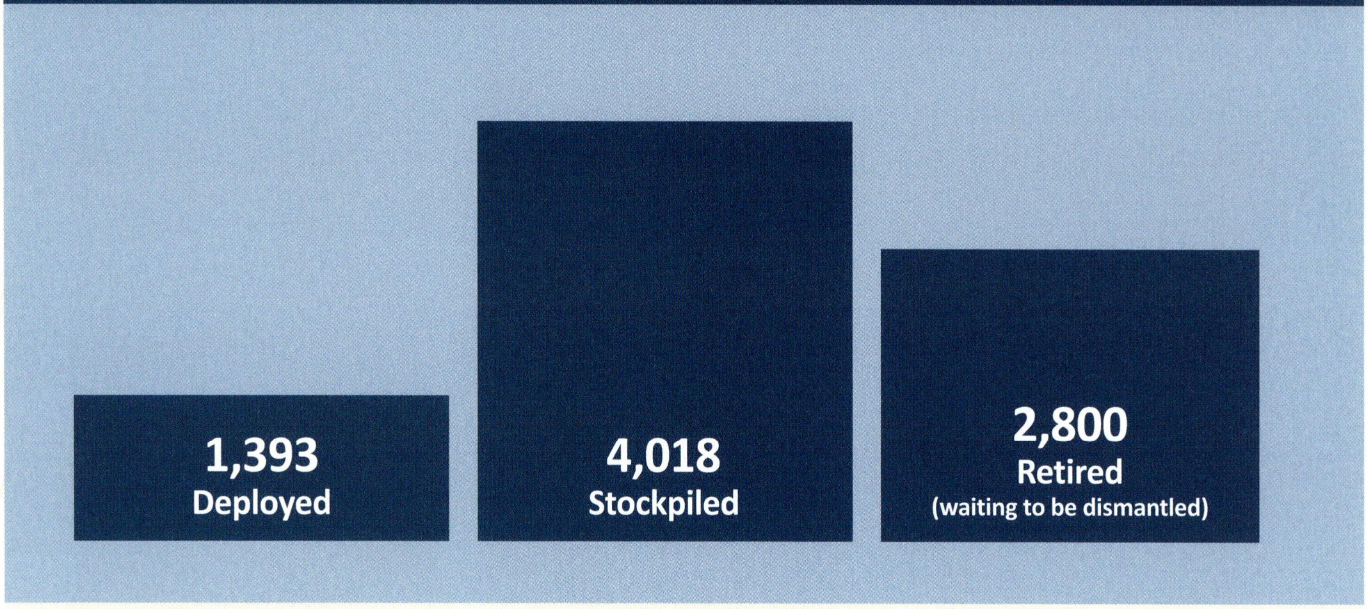

Reducing an Arsenal

The DOE and then the NNSA played the major role in safely getting rid of the number of nuclear warheads in the U.S. military. This process is called dismantling and disposition. Dismantling involves taking apart the warheads. Disposing means safely storing the radioactive parts.

Today workers at several different NNSA and DOE facilities are involved in dismantling and disposing old warheads. The work must be done carefully to prevent accidental explosions or the release of radiation. Scientists from the national labs that designed and built the nuclear elements help ensure the process is safe.

The NNSA removed nearly 1,000 pounds (450 kilograms) of highly enriched uranium-spent fuel from Poland as part of the Global Threat Reduction Initiative.

The United States has taken great steps to reduce its nuclear arsenal. But it still relies on it when considering the nation's military needs. That means some of the national labs must find ways to make sure old weapons will still function properly. It also means updating other weapons. Much of this work relies on the supercomputers at Los Alamos and Sandia National Laboratories in New Mexico and at Lawrence Livermore National Laboratory in California. One at Los Alamos, nicknamed Trinity, has a computing speed of 42 petaflops. The supercomputers allow lab scientists to predict how potent a warhead is without actually testing one.

One example of an updated nuclear weapon is the B61 bomb. It was first deployed in the 1960s to be dropped from planes. The two New Mexico labs are in charge of designing and testing a newer version of the bomb. Other DOE facilities also have a role in testing and then building the new bomb. It is due to be deployed in 2020.

Other duties of the NNSA include designing and building nuclear engines for about 80 U.S. Navy vessels. Most of them are submarines. With this work, scientists make sure the engines will operate safely at sea. The Navy does not want sailors exposed to harmful levels of radiation, especially in the tight space of a sub.

The NNSA is in charge of looking for nuclear devices that could be part of a terrorist attack. It also looks for other sources of radiation that pose a risk to Americans. The administration sends teams of experts around the world to deal with accidents. It offers medical aid when radiation has been released into the air or water.

The fear of terrorist groups buying or building a crude nuclear device increased after the September 11, 2001, attack on the United States. In 2011 one U.S. report said that a terrorist attack using such weapons posed the greatest risk to the world's safety. The NNSA is in charge of trying to keep nuclear weapons out of the hands of terrorists. The office works with other departments in the DOE, other U.S. agencies, and foreign nations to achieve that goal. One partnership with the Federal Bureau of Investigation (FBI) is Silent Thunder, a program that lets public officials, police officers, and others practice their response to a nuclear threat.

Disposal of nuclear materials, such as a dismantled B61 bomb, must be conducted meticulously to avoid radiation contamination and risk of nuclear theft.

Looking for "Dirty Bombs"

After 9/11 some U.S. officials worried that terrorists might acquire and use a nuclear device known as a dirty bomb. Such a weapon places regular explosives, such as dynamite, in a container with radioactive material. When it explodes, some radiation is released in the immediate area. A dirty bomb would not be particularly deadly compared to an actual nuclear weapon. The explosives would likely cause more deaths than the radiation would. But such a bomb would create fear and panic among Americans. In 2003, according to *The Washington Post*, the Department of Energy sent some of its scientists to five major cities to try to detect unexpected sources of radiation. They were looking for potential dirty bombs. The scientists hid their equipment in golf bags and briefcases so no one would suspect what they were doing. The scientists began their work shortly before New Year's Eve. They focused on public places where people would celebrate the coming of 2004. The only concern came in Las Vegas. The scientists found some radioactive material in a rented storage room. The government soon learned that the material was not part of a bomb plot.

Dirty bombs remain a concern today. Radioactive materials used to treat some cancers or waste from nuclear power plants could end up in the hands of terrorists looking to make a dirty bomb. That's why the DOE continues to improve security around radioactive materials and helps other countries try to stop their spread.

Proliferation refers to the unwanted increase and spread of nuclear devices. Part of the effort to prevent terrorists from developing or acquiring weapons means getting rid of radioactive material used around the world. The program to remove highly enriched uranium from nuclear reactors, as in Ghana, is part of that effort. So is finding better ways to detect and recover radioactive materials that have gone missing from labs and plants. To prevent that from happening, the NNSA's Office of Nonproliferation helps foreign countries improve their security to prevent thefts.

The Science of Energy

Along with the National Nuclear Security, another of the main parts of the DOE is the Office of the Undersecretary of Science. The undersecretary is chosen by the president and confirmed by the Senate. Within this department is a separate Office of Science that controls 10 of the 17 national laboratories. There, scientists focus on research related to sources of energy. The work at those labs extends into other topics too. They try to understand the nature of matter and energy across the universe. They look for ways to build faster supercomputers.

One energy issue that fascinates physicists is how to use nuclear fusion to generate power, as fission does. Fusion, or the combining of two things, is the process that provides the energy emitted by the sun and other stars. Fusion also creates the destructive power of the world's most powerful nuclear weapons. Using nuclear fusion to generate electricity would provide an unlimited source of energy without producing greenhouse gases. The Office of Science has an entire division that focuses on how to make fusion a safe source of power.

Much of the work on fusion involves the study of plasmas. They are often considered the fourth form of matter in the universe, after solids, liquids, and gases. The Northern Lights, which can be seen in parts of the world during the winter, are one example of plasma. In the lab, scientists can create plasmas by heating certain gases until some of the electrical particles inside their atoms change.

As part of its study of nuclear fusion and plasma, researchers from the Office of Science take part in an international project called ITER. The name comes from a Latin word meaning "the way." ITER has scientists from 35 countries working to perfect nuclear fusion as a source of energy. Working in France, they are building a device called a tokamak. Atoms in the plasma form of hydrogen fuse together inside of it, releasing heat. Magnets in the tokamak guide the movement of the plasma. The energy generated through this process can be used to heat water. The hot water creates steam to power turbines that generate electricity. ITER's tokamak, the largest in the world, is scheduled to be ready to test in 2025. Meanwhile, the Office of Science funds research at smaller, existing tokamaks.

Tokamaks were invented in the 1950s by Soviet scientists to produce controlled thermonuclear fusion power.

Department of Energy Helps Veterans

In 2017, eight of the DOE's national labs began putting their supercomputers to work on a new project. Along with the Department of Veterans Affairs (VA), the labs will process information about the nation's veterans in an effort to improve health care for them. The computers will analyze the health records of some 24 million veterans that the VA has collected over the past 20 years. The VA has also collected genetic information on hundreds of thousands of vets. Genes are chemicals in cells that shape a person's physical traits. Certain genes can also increase a person's risk of developing some diseases. The scientists involved in the project hope that by feeding the health data into the supercomputers they can learn what factors increase veterans' risks for developing diseases such as cancer. The information should also be able to help Americans who did not serve in the military. Frank Alexander works at Brookhaven National Laboratory, one of the national labs taking part. He said, "Each lab possesses varying computational expertise. The DOE labs are here to help solve complex national problems, so we are all very excited about this opportunity to help our veterans."

Another key department within the Office of the Undersecretary of Science is the Office of Environmental Management. It is in charge of cleaning up the sites where the United States built its first nuclear weapons and carried out nuclear research. As of 2018, Environmental Management was working at 107 sites across the nation.

A cleanup is underway at the Hanford Nuclear Reservation near Richland, Washington, where nuclear production occurred during the Manhattan Project.

The Department of Energy created the Office of Environmental Management in 1989. That year one of the largest cleanup projects began at the nuclear facility in Hanford, Washington. For decades it produced fuel for nuclear reactors and material for nuclear weapons. Radioactive material from the facility came from metal parts, from clothing workers wore, and from wastewater that leaked into the ground or was stored in large tanks. As of August 2017 the DOE had removed harmful materials from 18 billion gallons (68 billion liters) of water and cleaned up about 85 percent of the land at the facility. The Office of Legacy Management plans to take over managing the site in the future.

The third major division within the DOE is the Office of the Undersecretary of Energy. Smaller offices within it focus on forms of energy currently available. These include renewable sources, such as wind and solar power, nuclear energy, and fossil fuels. Another office focuses on energy issues for Indian tribes and villages. Its programs help bring electricity to rural areas. It also helps tribal nations develop sources of energy on their lands. One emphasis is on increasing solar and wind power on those lands. One office within the division also addresses such issues as worker safety, environmental concerns, and security related to activities done at DOE facilities and by its contractors.

The Campo Indian Reservation along the border of California and Mexico uses wind turbines to produce electricity.

CHAPTER FOUR

The Department of Energy Today and Tomorrow

In 2015 representatives from almost 200 nations met in Paris to discuss climate change. Major industrial nations, including the United States, agreed to cut their production of the greenhouse gases that contribute to global warming. Many of these gases come from the use of coal and petroleum. Scientists around the world warned that if the emissions of those gases continued to increase, global temperatures could warm to dangerous levels. With the agreement, the world's richest nations also agreed to help poorer countries use fewer fossil fuels and develop cleaner sources of energy.

President Barack Obama went to Paris to show U.S. support for the agreement. After he returned home, he said that since he had taken office in 2009, his administration had "transformed the United States into the global leader in fighting climate change." The next year, the United States formally entered the agreement.

In the United States, the Paris Agreement meant the Department of Energy would play a major role in reducing the use of fossil fuels. The DOE would also give more support to energy sources that did not create greenhouse gases. In October 2016 Secretary of Energy Ernest Moniz said the agreement would mean new jobs in the United States tied to the development of the clean energy sources. He said, "America has the workers, the entrepreneurs, the scientists, the engineers, and the desire to be the global . . . leader for clean energy technology, research, development, and [use]."

Nuclear physicist Ernest Moniz served as Secretary of Energy during the Obama administration.

As Moniz made those remarks, Hillary Clinton and Donald Trump were running for president. Clinton supported the Paris Agreement, but Trump did not. He didn't think that climate change was a real threat to Earth. Earlier he had called the idea a hoax. In 2016 he said he didn't think humans added to the problem. He also believed that cutting the use of coal and oil would hurt the U.S. industries that produced those fuels. Trump won the election in 2016. In June 2017 he announced that the United States would pull out of the Paris Agreement.

Trump's secretary of Energy, Rick Perry, said, "President Trump's decision will prove to be the right course of action and one I fully support." Trump said his administration would consider trying to create a new agreement that was more favorable to the U.S. economy. Several European leaders, however, rejected the idea of making a new agreement.

The changing of presidential administrations in the United States often leads to big changes in the policies and direction of executive departments. Trump's election meant a new direction for the Department of Energy, as the president's action on the Paris Agreement showed. Rick Perry had called for getting rid of the DOE when he ran for president in 2012. He, like Trump, favored finding and using as much fossil fuel as possible. Under the department's budget for 2018, Trump also called for cutting the amount of money spent to develop renewable energy.

President Donald Trump appointed former Texas governor Rick Perry as Secretary of Energy in 2017.

Ending Efforts to Address Climate Change

Even before the Paris Agreement of 2015, one part of the DOE was working with foreign countries to try to combat global warming. The Office of International Climate and Technology was started in 2010 to help countries find ways to reduce their emissions of carbon dioxide and other greenhouse gases. For example, the office worked with officials in India to increase the use of light bulbs that required less energy. India relies on coal to generate most of its electricity and is one the world's largest producers of greenhouse gases. A DOE official under Barack Obama said the light bulb program "will lead to massive savings in terms of avoided carbon dioxide emissions and air pollution." The Office of International Climate and Technology also helped organize an annual international meeting that explored new ways to reduce greenhouse gases. Under Donald Trump, the DOE shut down the office. The move was part of a larger Trump effort to stop funding all the department's programs specifically related to climate change. Trump wanted to keep the nation focused on fossil fuels for its energy needs. He believed this helped create jobs and bring in money from fuels sold overseas. Along with that came his efforts to reduce spending on the alternative fuels, even as many people argued they would help fight global warming.

Tug of War over Clean Power

In the years since the DOE was first created, the cost of renewable energy sources has fallen. By 2017, in about 30 countries, electricity generated by the sun and wind cost the same as that generated by fossil fuels. The gap between the two sources of power has also fallen dramatically in the United States. Another major change from the 1970s was the discovery of new sources of natural gas and petroleum in the United States. By 2018 the nation was the world's leading producer of both oil and natural gas.

When it comes to energy issues, the Trump administration's DOE differs from President Obama's in several specific ways. As part of the effort to reduce harmful gas emissions, Obama proposed what he called the Clean Power Plan. It focused on reducing the use of coal to generate the nation's electricity. Coal-fired plants produce large amounts of the gases that are linked to global warming, such as carbon dioxide and sulfur dioxide. While the amount of emissions had fallen since the 1990s, Obama wanted them reduced even more.

Donald Trump had run for president promising to help coal companies mine and sell more coal. As part of that effort, his administration announced in October 2017 that it was ending the Clean Power Plan. The future of coal as an energy source, however, remained uncertain. The DOE had prepared a report earlier in the year that said the lower cost of natural gas was making coal less desirable as a fuel at electrical power plants. Many coal-fired plants had already been shut across the nation because of cheaper natural gas. Increased use of solar and wind power was also affecting the use of coal. Still, DOE Secretary Rick Perry called for new rules that would require electricity customers to spend money that would keep some coal plants operating. In 2018 the DOE said electric companies should buy power from older coal plants for two years, while the department studied the security of the nation's production of electricity.

Perry's proposal called for giving similar support to some nuclear power plants as well. Many Americans had worried about the safety of those plants after the Three Mile Island accident in 1979. Worries increased after serious accidents took place in the Soviet Union (1986) and Japan (2011). The United States, however, had continued to use nuclear power for some of its energy needs. During the early 2000s several companies proposed building new nuclear plants. Under Obama, the DOE supported research on nuclear power and generating it safely. It also set aside money for loans to build new plants. But nuclear plants, like those that use coal, were hurt by the low price of natural gas. And new plants under construction in Georgia and South Carolina cost much more than originally planned.

The most serious nuclear accident in U.S. history happened on March 28, 1979, when a nuclear reactor melted down at Three Mile Island power plant.

Under Trump the DOE strongly supports the use of nuclear energy. Perry said, "One of the things we want to do at DOE is to make nuclear energy cool again." Both he and Trump stressed that nuclear power plants do not emit harmful gases. But they are expensive and they do have safety concerns relating to radiation.

The Trump administration also brought in new ideas about where to drill for oil. Since the 1970s, a region of Alaska called the North Slope has produced hundreds of millions of barrels of oil. Oil companies, Republican lawmakers that support the companies, and some lawmakers in Alaska also called for drilling in the nearby Arctic National Wildlife Refuge. The area had been set aside to protect such animals as caribou and polar bears. Opponents of drilling in the refuge have argued that the

Environmental activists are against drilling for oil in places like the Arctic National Wildlife Refuge, where caribou and other animals live.

The Trans-Alaskan oil pipeline is 800 miles (1,300 kilometers) long and is one of the world's largest pipeline systems.

work could threaten the lives of those and other animals. Some Native Alaskans, particularly from the Gwich'in Nation, are concerned. They rely on the refuge's caribou for meat. Only Congress has the legal power to allow drilling in the refuge, but the Trump administration voiced its support for it. Secretary Perry had earlier indicated that he also backed drilling there, and at the end of 2017, Congress voted to allow drilling in the refuge as part of the Tax Cuts and Jobs Act.

The Trump administration also called for more drilling off the coast of the United States. In 2018 the administration said it wanted to loosen old rules on where companies could drill and let oil companies drill at new sites along the coast.

The DOE under Trump also called for an increase in fracking. This process lets companies bring more petroleum and natural gas out of the ground. Fracking was the major reason why the United States became a world leader in producing those fossil fuels. The Department of Energy funded some of the first projects that helped develop fracking technology. At the end of 2017 the Trump administration announced it would end the limitation of fracking on federal lands. At about the same time, the DOE announced it would give $30 million to help several small companies with fracking projects.

Not all issues and programs relating to energy and the DOE change when a new president takes office. Both Obama and Trump supported the work at the national labs directed at improving the nation's nuclear weapons. Obama called for spending more money on the work, and in 2016 almost $9 billion went to that effort. In its first budget under Trump, the DOE called for increasing that amount by $1.4 billion.

Concerns over the safety of the nation's nuclear weapons program have also been a constant. Part of the problem has been the work done by contractors the DOE hires to run the labs and clean up old nuclear sites. They often try to save money by not following safety rules. Other times the rules are broken out of carelessness. At Los Alamos National Laboratory in 2017, workers mishandled plutonium, exposing some of them to radiation. That year a DOE official in charge of investigating problems within the department noted the safety concerns at many DOE sites. The department also must deal with safely getting rid of millions of gallons of liquid and large amounts of solid nuclear waste. The estimated cost for doing this work is more than $50 billion.

Looking ahead, the DOE under Trump and future presidents will continue to face challenges related to nuclear weapons and waste, energy production, and global warming. The issues are complex and sometimes even people within the administration don't agree. One example came in 2017 with the release of a report that said climate change was largely caused by human activity. Scientists from DOE and other federal departments helped write it. Although the conclusion did not agree with what Trump had said about climate change, his administration released the report.

Large supplies of fuel to create energy are key for keeping the United States growing. Creating that energy without risking lives or the environment is a goal for many people across the nation. The Department of Energy will play a key role in finding new ways to address that goal.

President Trump and Secretary Perry support using nuclear power as an energy source for the future and call for funding nuclear power plants around the country.

What You Can Do

If you're concerned about an issue that involves the Department of Energy, you can write the lawmakers who represent you in Congress. Congress often holds meetings to question DOE officials on their policies, and the lawmakers can sometimes influence what the DOE does. This link will help you find the member of the House of Representatives for where you live:

https://www.house.gov/representatives/find-your-representative

This link shows the current members of the U.S. Senate. Each state has two senators:

https://www.senate.gov/senators/contact/

The DOE also encourages the public to offer comments on proposed rules. Use the link below to get more information.

https://www.energy.gov/eere/buildings/how-participate-or-comment

I will be worthy
of trust.

Timeline

1910

The U.S. government creates the Bureau of Mines to improve safety in coal mines.

1920

The Federal Power Commission is created to help oversee the building of hydroelectric dams.

1945

The United States drops two atomic bombs on Japan.

1954

The U.S. Navy launches the first vessel powered by nuclear energy; Congress passes the Atomic Energy Act, which lets private companies research peaceful uses of nuclear power.

1957

The United States opens the first commercial nuclear power plant to generate electricity.

1973

An oil embargo cuts supplies of gasoline and drives up the prices.

1977

Congress creates the Department of Energy (DOE) and President Jimmy Carter selects James Schlesinger as its first secretary.

1979

An accident at the Three Mile Island nuclear power plant slows the growth of nuclear-powered electrical plants in the United States.

2001

Terrorists attacks on the United States raise the fear of terrorists trying to buy or build nuclear weapons.

2003

The Office of Legacy Management is created within the DOE to oversee the cleanup of sites with nuclear waste.

2015

President Barack Obama supports the Paris Agreement, which calls on the nation to reduce its emission of greenhouse gases.

2017

President Donald Trump announces that he will pull the United States out of the Paris Agreement in 2020.

2018

The United States is the world's leading producer of petroleum and natural gas.

Glossary

administration–a specific department or agency within a government, or the total of the people and departments controlled by a U.S. president

atom–a tiny particle that together with other atoms makes up every substance

budget–a plan of what someone thinks they will spend

commercial–relating to efforts to sell goods or services to make a profit

contractor–a business or individual hired to carry out a specific job

embargo–the halting of sales of certain goods to certain customers

emission–a chemical, particularly a gas, released into the air

enriched–something containing added material to make it more useful

extract–to remove something from its source

fission–the splitting apart of atoms to release energy

fossil fuel–a fuel such as natural gas and oil that formed in the ground millions of years ago from dead, rotting plants and animals

hydroelectric–relating to the use of moving water to generate electricity

nonproliferation–to prevent the increase or spread of countries possessing nuclear weapons

nuclear–relating to the nucleus, or center, of an atom

reactor–a device that contains radioactive material used to create nuclear power

renewable–from a source that will never run out

turbine–a machine with large blades that spin to produce energy

Additional Resources

Critical Thinking

1. Describe one of the events during the 1970s that led the U.S. government to create the Department of Energy.

2. Based on the arguments for and against using nuclear power, do you think the United States should support the building of more nuclear energy plants? Why or why not?

3. Explain one of the ways the Department of Energy's national labs help strengthen the country's military defense.

Further Reading

Gitlin, Marty. *The Arms Race and Nuclear Proliferation.* New York: Greenhaven Publishing, 2018.

Heos, Bridget. *It's Getting Hot in Here: The Past, the Present, and the Future of Global Warming.* Boston: HMH Books for Young Readers, 2016.

Honders, Christine. *Nuclear Power Plants: Harnessing the Power of Nuclear Energy.* New York: PowerKids Press, 2018.

Labrecque, Ellen. *Renewable Energy.* Ann Arbor, MI: Cherry Lake Publishing, 2018.

Sherman, Jill. *Fossil Fuels.* New York: Enslow Publishing, 2018.

Internet Sites

Use Facthound to find Internet sites related to this book.

Visit www.facthound.com

Just type in 9780756559007 and go.

Source Notes

p. 8, "To ensure America's security and prosperity..." U.S. Department of Energy. Department of Energy Mission, https://energy.gov/mission Accessed on November 20, 2017.

p. 12, "Now I hope to help..." Ariana Tantillo, "Bringing Diversity into Computational Science Through Student Outreach." Brookhaven National Laboratory, September 28, 2017, https://www.bnl.gov/newsroom/news.php?a=212478 Accessed on December 12, 2017.

p. 27, "We cannot take our energy supply..." Richard Nixon, Special Message to the Congress on Energy Resources, June 4, 1971. The American Presidency Project, http://www.presidency.ucsb.edu/ws/?pid=3038 Accessed on December 18, 2017.

p. 30, "make sure that consumers of our country..." Jimmy Carter, Department of Energy Organization Act and Bill Amending the Small Business Administration Act Remarks on Signing S. 826 and H.R. 692 into Law, August 4, 1977. The American Presidency Project, http://www.presidency.ucsb.edu/ws/index.php?pid=7916&st=energy&st1= Accessed on December 18, 2017.

p. 43, "Each lab possesses..." Jane Koropsak, "Brookhaven Lab Partners with Seven U.S. Department of Energy Labs to Support and Enhance Medical Data Analysis for U.S. Veterans." Brookhaven National Laboratory, November 13, 2017. https://www.bnl.gov/newsroom/news.php?a=212574 Accessed on December 21, 2017.

p. 46, "transformed the United States..." Statement by the President on the Paris Climate Agreement, Obama White House Archives, December 12, 2015. https://obamawhitehouse.archives.gov/the-press-office/2015/12/12/statement-president-paris-climate-agreement Accessed on January 6, 2018.

p. 47, "America has the workers..." Secretary Moniz Statement on Reaching Threshold for Paris Agreement's Entry into Force, Department of Energy, October 5, 2016. https://energy.gov/articles/secretary-moniz-statement-reaching-threshold-paris-agreement-s-entry-force Accessed on January 6, 2018.

p. 48, "President Trump's decision will prove..." Statement by Secretary Rick Perry on President Trump's Announcement Regarding the Paris Accord, Department of Energy, June 1, 2017. https://energy.gov/articles/statement-secretary-rick-perry-president-trumps-announcement-regarding-paris-accord Accessed on January 6, 2018.

p. 49, "will lead to massive savings..." Brad Plumer, "Energy Department Closes Office Working on Climate Change Abroad," *The New York Times*, June 15, 2017. Available online at https://www.nytimes.com/2017/06/15/climate/energy-department-closes-office-working-on-climate-change-abroad.html?_r=0 Accessed on January 7, 2018.

p. 52, "One of the things..." "Trump Puts Nuclear First on America's Energy Agenda," Nuclear Energy Institute, June 29, 2017. https://www.nei.org/News-Media/News/News-Archives/2017/Trump-Puts-Nuclear-First-on-America-s-Energy-Agend Accessed on January 7, 2018.

Select Bibliography

Department of Energy Websites, including:
https://science.energy.gov/lp/strategic-partnership-projects
https://energy.gov/eere/wipo/about-state-energy-program
https://www.energy.gov/fy-2017-department-energy-budget-request-fact-sheet
https://nnsa.energy.gov/mediaroom/pressreleases/trinity
https://www.netl.doe.gov/about/netl-history
https://energy.gov/sites/prod/files/AEC%20History.pdf
https://energy.gov/sites/prod/files/FEA%20History.pdf
https://nnsa.energy.gov/aboutus/ourprograms/defenseprograms
https://science.energy.gov/
https://www.energy.gov/sites/prod/files/FEA%20History.pdf

Administrative Law Review, Vol. 30, No. 2 (Spring 1978), pp. 193-236.

Byse, Clark. "The Department of Energy Organization Act: Structure and Procedure.

Feldman, Michael. "Oak Ridge Readies Summit Supercomputer for 2018 Debut." Top 500, November 15, 2017. https://www.top500.org/news/oak-ridge-readies-summit-supercomputer-for-2018-debut/ Accessed on December 8, 2017.

Greenhouse Gas Emissions. Environmental Protection Agency, https://www.epa.gov/ghgemissions/overview-greenhouse-gases#carbon-dioxide Accessed on January 3, 2018.

History. U.S. Nuclear Regulatory Commission, https://www.nrc.gov/about-nrc/emerg-preparedness/history.html Accessed on November 28, 2017.

Natural Gas Extraction - Hydraulic Fracturing. Environmental Protection Agency. https://www.epa.gov/hydraulicfracturing Accessed on December 14, 2017.

Nixon, Richard. Address to the Nation About Policies to Deal With the Energy Shortages, November 7, 1973. The American Presidency Project, http://www.presidency.ucsb.edu/ws/index.php?pid=4034&st=project+independence&st1 Accessed on December 18, 2017.

Nixon, Richard. Special Message to the Congress on Energy Resources, June 4, 1971. The American Presidency Project, http://www.presidency.ucsb.edu/ws/?pid=3038 Accessed on December 18, 2017.

"NNSA Removes All Highly Enriched Uranium from Ghana." National Nuclear Security Administration, August 29, 2017. https://nnsa.energy.gov/mediaroom/pressreleases/nnsa-removes-all-highly-enriched-uranium-ghana Accessed on December 18, 2017.

U.S. Energy Facts, Explained. U.S. Energy Information Administration, https://www.eia.gov/energyexplained/?page=us_energy_home Accessed on December 5, 2017.

Index

About the Author

Michael Burgan has written numerous books for children and young adults during his nearly 25 years as a freelance writer. Many of his books have focused on U.S. history, geography, and the lives of world leaders. Michael has won several awards for his writing, and his graphic novel version of the classic tale *Frankenstein* (Capstone) was a Junior Library Guild selection. Michael graduated from the University of Connecticut with a bachelor's degree in history. He lives in Santa Fe, New Mexico, with his cat, Callie.